When Moms and Kids Have ADD

Patricia O. Quinn, M.D.
Kathleen G. Nadeau, Ph.D.

EXPANDED VERSION

ADVANTAGE BOOKS

Washington, DC

Library of Congress Cataloging-in-Publication Data

Quinn, Patricia O.
When moms and kids have ADD (ADHD) / Patricia O. Quinn, Kathleen G. Nadeau.
p.cm. — (ADD-friendly living)
Includes bibliographical references.
ISBN 0-9714609-1-4
1. Attention-deficit disordered children—Family relationships. 2. Attention-deficit disordered adults—Family relationships. 3. Mother and child. I. Nadeau, Kathleen G. II. Title. III. Series

RJ506.H9Q5483 2004
649'.154—dc22

2004062391

Published by
ADVANTAGE BOOKS, LLC
3268 Arcadia Place, NW
Washington, DC 20015
888-238-8588

10 9 8 7 6 5 4 3 2
Printed in the U.S.A.

The term ADD is used for simplicity in this book and is intended to stand for Attention Deficit Hyperactivity Disorder and to include all aspects of the disorder including the hyperactive as well as non-hyperactive type.

The material presented in this book is intended for informational purposes only and should not be considered a substitute for medical or psychological advice.

Welcome to our ADD-FRIENDLY LIVING SERIES!

When you or a member of your family is diagnosed with ADD, the first question often asked is, "What can I do about it?" This series is designed to answer that question. Each volume in our series will focus on one aspect of ADD – providing specific tools, tips and strategies for parents, adults, couples or families, helping them learn to live in a more ADD-friendly way – with more satisfaction and less stress.

What is ADD (ADHD)?

Attention Deficit Disorder (ADD or ADHD) is a chronic neurobiological disorder that impairs attention, concentration and organizational skills. It can affect every aspect of a person's life and commonly persists into adulthood. Living with ADD can be challenging, but it can also be very rewarding. The key to success is to understand how to adjust your behaviors, habits and lifestyle to meet your ADD needs.

As the terms ADD or ADHD became more familiar during the 1990s, many books were written about Attention Deficit Disorder (for simplicity's sake, we'll use the term ADD). Most focused on how to diagnose ADD and on the medications used in treatment, but very few books provided information on ways that individuals and their families could take charge of the many challenges of ADD and lead productive and fulfilling lives.

ADD-friendly living . . .

ADD affects every aspect of life and every aspect of life has an effect upon ADD. Where you live, how you live and the people you encounter on a daily basis can all affect the challenges of ADD for better or worse.

Our goal in this series is to help people with ADD and their families make changes in their daily living patterns and in their environment that will create a more ADD-friendly lifestyle. In particular, we hope to teach people how to work with their ADD instead of always fighting against it.

ADD-friendly books . . .

The **ADD-FRIENDLY LIVING SERIES** books are designed with the ADD reader in mind. Too often, books on ADD go unread because they are so ADD-unfriendly. Either they are not relevant to one's situation, too long, too cluttered or too boring – causing a reader with ADD to quickly lose interest.

Our goal in this series is to create information-packed books that an individual with ADD *will* read because they:

- **Focus** on a single topic;
- **Get to the point,** so that information can be found quickly;
- **Are well-organized,** with bold topic headings and bulleted lists;
- **Are reader-friendly,** with clear print and eye-catching graphics; and
- **Provide summaries** for quick review.

We hope that our **ADD-FRIENDLY LIVING SERIES** will help our readers create a more ADD-friendly lifestyle for themselves and those they love.

Initial printing for this first volume of our **ADD-FRIENDLY LIVING SERIES** was produced in partnership with The National Center for Gender Issues and ADHD, a not-for-profit organization dedicated to raising awareness of and advocating for women with ADHD, and was supported by an educational grant from Eli Lilly & Company. This revised and expanded, second edition is published by **Advantage Books, LLC.**

For more information on ADD-friendly living, visit:
www.addvance.com.

> *"If you help a mother love her life, you will help a family. And as families go, so goes society."*
> — Dr. Brenda Hunter

When Moms and Kids Have ADD

Patricia Quinn, M.D. and Kathleen Nadeau, Ph.D.

Parenting is a difficult role for which few of us are trained. When Attention Deficit Disorder is added to the mix, parenting becomes even more challenging. Many mothers have come to us over the years, frustrated because they cannot find adequate resources to guide them in dealing with their own ADD.

A number of books have been written about raising a child with ADD, but the parenting advice they offer is often inappropriate when the mother has ADD as well. One mother with ADD succinctly described her challenge, asking, "How am I supposed to organize my child when I can't even organize myself?"

Our goal in writing this parenting guide is to provide solutions for mothers with ADD who often feel overwhelmed by the challenging job of raising kids with ADD.

The advice you'll find here takes into account that moms with ADD need support too. Moms need to learn to manage their own ADD before they can be successful in helping their child meet the challenges of ADD.

Instead of placing the primary parenting burden on the mother, our guidelines suggest ways to create an ADD-friendly family environment – an environment that minimizes the negative impact of ADD and nurtures the gifts and talents of each family member.

ADD is a family affair. Everyone is affected when several family members have ADD, and all need to work together to create an environment in which each family member can feel and function better. Instead of only focusing on a child's ADD problem-behaviors, our guidelines will help mothers to find creative solutions that involve the entire family.

Guideline No. 1

To take good care of your child, first take good care of yourself.

If you are a mother with ADD, your first step should be to get treatment for yourself. A mother's usual tendency is to focus on her child's difficulties while neglecting her own. Just as the airline flight attendant instructs you to put on your own oxygen mask before assisting your child, you must first get help for your own ADD before you can effectively deal with your child's problems.

A recent study suggests that parent training programs are not very helpful when the mother has untreated ADD, lending even more weight to the importance of treatment for women with ADD.

For more information about ADD in women, check out the following:

- *Understanding Women with AD/HD* by Kathleen Nadeau and Patricia Quinn
- *Gender Issues and AD/HD* by Patricia Quinn and Kathleen Nadeau
- *Women with ADD* by Sari Solden
- www.addvance.com
- www.ncgiadd.org

Guideline No. 2

Look for a professional who understands ADD in women.

If you are a woman seeking diagnosis and treatment, you may need to make an extra effort to find a professional who can give you the help you need. Many professionals overlook or misdiagnose ADD in girls and women because it sometimes looks different than it does in boys and men.

Keep in mind:

- **Misdiagnosis of women with ADD is common.** Studies show that as a woman with ADD, you are more likely to be misdiagnosed with anxiety or depression.

- **Anxiety or depression may be part of the ADD picture, but not the whole picture.** Treating anxiety and depression doesn't address the feeling of being overwhelmed or the disorganization that results from having ADD.

- **Women with ADD need to self-advocate.** Educate yourself about ADD. Armed with this information, you will be better able to discuss your symptoms with a professional who may know little about how ADD presents in women. If you can not find a professional who is already experienced in treating women, look for one that is open to learning more. Let them know about books, articles and resources that are available for women and girls with ADD. (See resources p.12)

Guideline No. 3

Don't shortchange yourself when you seek treatment – effective treatment usually involves a variety of interventions and supports.

Among adults, ADD rarely occurs alone. There are many conditions that frequently co-occur with ADD. Effective treatment for ADD should also focus on any related conditions you may have, such as anxiety and depression.

Look for therapists, coaches and organizers who can work with you and your family to create a more ADD-friendly home environment. While symptoms of ADD often quickly respond to medication, effective treatment for all aspects of ADD can be a complex process. There are no easy answers. At various times, you may need to focus on different issues that require parent or couples counseling, coaching and/or the help of a professional organizer.

Professional organizers can be located through the National Association of Professional Organizers at **www.napo.net**.

ADD coaches can be found through a number of organizations including:

www.americoach.org	**www.nancyratey.com**
www.addcoaching.com	**www.add.org**
www.addconsults.com	**www.addresources.org**

Guideline No. 4

Build a network of support.

Find or form a women's ADD support group. Sharing your struggle with a group of women who understand can be a very helpful, healing experience.

Seek out allies who are ADD-friendly – people who are not hypercritical or competitive; people who see your gifts and understand your ADD.

Get the support that you need. You may need more support to manage your daily life than a woman without ADD. Look for creative ways to find support.

Arrange for a mother's helper. To manage your own ADD and to be a calm and

An excellent source of online support for women with ADD is **www.flylady.net** – a website that provides online personal coaching for women.

Many women's ADD support groups have developed across the country. To find a support group near you, try searching the Internet using **www.google.com** or **www.yahoo.com.**

Some women's ADD support groups are listed at **www.addvance.com.**

consistent mother, you'll need regular breaks from being "on-duty" with the kids.

Anticipate high-stress times – for example your PMS week or times when your partner is away – and plan ahead for extra support from a babysitter, a mother's helper or a friend.

Emphasize your gifts, the things you love to do. Find others who can join with you in making these positive experiences a greater part of your life.

Guideline No. 5

Reduce stress in order to reduce ADD challenges.

As stress increases, ADD symptoms tend to increase for both you and your child. Symptoms such as disorganization, forgetfulness and poor management of daily tasks are often magnified by stress. But the reverse is also true. When you reduce stress in your life, ADD becomes easier to manage.

- **Do a stress-analysis of your daily life.**

    Make a list of the things that cause stress – both large and small.

- **Then use this list as a guide for reducing stress.**

    For example, you might consider:

    - Reducing your commitments;

    - Changing spending patterns to get out of debt;

    - Getting more sleep and exercise;

    - Simplifying your daily patterns; or

    - Spending more time with supportive people.

More information on reducing stress for adults with ADD can be found in:
Adventures in Fast Forward
by Kathleen Nadeau (see resources)

Guideline No. 6

Simplify your life.

In today's fast-paced world, every woman looks for ways to simplify her life. As a woman with ADD, your need to cut back is even greater. Here are some ideas to get started:

- Get rid of items you don't really use.
- Choose low-maintenance clothing for the whole family.
- Select sturdy family-friendly home furnishings.
- Look for easy ways to increase household order. Do you need coat hooks in the entryway? More storage in the kids' rooms? A storage bin to neatly store bottles and newspapers for recycling?
- Develop simple weekday menus.
- Reduce the number of newspaper and magazine subscriptions.
- Decrease the commitments of each family member.
- Get your kids involved in finding creative ways to "keep it simple."

Real Simple Magazine (available by subscription, in supermarkets and on newsstands) offers great suggestions on simplifying your life.

Look online for websites that offer items to help organize your space and store belongings, such as:

- **www.organizedliving.com**
- **www.containerstore.com**
- **www.holdeverything.com**

Guideline No. 7

To be at your best as a mother, make time for yourself.

It's rare for a mom with ADD to get a moment to herself. The day goes by in a blur of getting the kids off to school, work, carpooling, kids' activities, meals, and homework. When she finally has a few quiet moments at the end of the day, it's very tempting to eat (sometimes compulsively), watch TV, surf the internet, or dive into a good book, only to realize a few hours later that, once again, she has stayed up far past her bedtime and will face the next day feeling unprepared and exhausted. What to do?

- **First, don't feel guilty!** You need time to relax and get off the daily treadmill.

- **Make it a top priority to get your kids to bed on time.**
  Many women with ADD lose track of time in the evening, or
  may feel "too tired" to get the kids started on their bedtime
  routine. As a result, their children stay up far later than they
  should. This leads moms to stay up even later, snatching a few
  moments of relaxation that can stretch into a few hours. The
  result? The family wakes up late, tired, and disorganized most
  mornings.

- **Get ready for bed first.** Just like your kids, your evenings
  will go more smoothly, and your mornings too, if you follow a
  bedtime routine. Both you and your kids should complete
  your "bedtime routine" before getting involved in TV, reading,
  or the internet. Get yourself organized for the next day – set
  out clothes, or at least decide what you'll wear. Shower, brush
  your teeth and put on your nightgown or pajamas. Now it's
  "me time" – those precious moments of relaxation.

- **Set a bedtime for yourself!** It's not just your kids that need
  sleep – you need sleep just as badly. So set a bedtime and
  look for ways to make sure you meet it. If you have a partner,
  ask for a 10 minute warning when it's time to get in bed.

- **Use an alarm clock to get yourself to sleep!** If you don't
  have a partner, set an alarm clock that reminds you when to
  go to bed. Don't hit the snooze button more than once!

- **Look for ways to build moments of relaxation into
  daytime hours.** Women who are deprived of "me time" all
  day long are more likely to over-do it at night. It's a lot like
  eating – you're more likely to binge at night if you haven't
  eaten much during the day.

Guideline No. 8

Help your child learn about ADD from a positive, constructive perspective.

Many parents are uncomfortable telling their child about ADD. Some fear that the ADD "label" will make their child feel bad. Others simply don't know what to tell their child.

As a mother who has lived with ADD all of her life, you know that it can be very difficult to grow up with untreated ADD. Most children recognize that they are different and blame themselves. They may believe that they are "stupid" or "bad" because they are forgetful, can't pay attention or remember as easily as their classmates.

Telling your child about your own ADD can be the beginning of positive change. Teach your child that with the right kind of help they can feel better and function better at home and at school.

Good information on how to tell your child about ADD can be found in:

- *Learning to Slow Down and Pay Attention* by Kathleen Nadeau and Ellen Dixon
- *Putting on the Brakes* by Patricia Quinn and Judith Stern
  (see resources)

Guideline No. 9

Become an ADD role model for your child.

When you take charge of your ADD, you help both yourself and your child. Share your efforts, your successes and your frustrations. Talk about the problem-solving that you do to manage ADD challenges. Let your child know that the best approach to ADD challenges is to attack the problem instead of attacking oneself. This is a good way to teach your child a positive, responsible and realistic view of how to manage with ADD.

Give your child an ADD role model of self-acceptance and personal responsibility. Together, you and your children can tackle ADD challenges with humor and mutual support.

Guideline No. 10

Work together as a family to meet the challenges of ADD.

- **Tackle ADD as a family.** Learn about ADD together and set family goals for getting organized and solving the problems of daily life.

- **Give yourself and your family a break!** Let go of unrealistic expectations and set goals that are right for you and your family.

- **Approach ADD foibles** in yourself and in other family members with humor.

- **Take care of your own and your family's health.** Exercising and playing together, eating nutritious family meals and getting the whole family to bed on time can help reduce the negative impact of ADD.

More information on ways to work together as a family can be found in:
Adventures in Fast Forward by Kathleen Nadeau
(see resources)

Guideline No. 11

Create an ADD-friendly family.

An ADD-friendly family is one that solves problems and celebrates successes together. How can your family become more ADD-friendly? Here are some ideas:

- **Focus on what's important** – being loving, encouraging and cooperative.

- **Don't sweat the details**, like who left the wet towel on the floor.

> More information on creating an ADD-friendly family can be found in:
> - *Adventures in Fast Forward* by Kathleen Nadeau
> - *Help4ADD@HighSchool* by Kathleen Nadeau
>
> (see resources)

- **Be patient with each other.** It's easier to keep trying when you feel that your family is behind you.

- **Learn to laugh** over ADD-related dilemmas. Humor eases the way through inevitable daily glitches.

- **Spend time enjoying each other.** Don't just focus on problems.

- **Accommodate family forgetfulness** with notes, message centers and user-friendly reminders.

- **Create a family philosophy** that it's OK to be different from one another.

- **Make home a safe haven** – a place where each family member feels loved and supported.

Guideline No. 12

Remember, non-squeaky wheels need oil too! Don't overlook the needs of your non-ADD child.

It's easy to become so caught up in meeting ADD challenges that you overlook the needs of your non-ADD child. However, going too long without oiling the "non-squeaky" wheel in the family can create a different set of problems. She may become angry, feeling that excuses are made for her ADD sib, or resentful that she receives too little of your time and attention. It's never easy to give everyone the time and attention they need (and, remember, your own needs are important too), but here are some tips:

■ **Make a date with your non-ADD child** – Remember, as a mom with ADD, it's easy to get caught up in the reactive mode; and ADD children are often masters at causing reactions! To guard against short-changing a less demanding child, make regular "dates" to spend time together, just the two of you. These "dates" don't need to be long or complicated, just regular times that make your non-ADD child feel special and noticed.

■ **Don't expect too much self-control from your non-ADD child.** Living with an often provocative ADD-sibling can be very challenging.

- **Let your non-ADD child know you're aware of the challenges of living with a sib who has ADD.** A simple word of acknowledgment can go a long way to making things better.

- **Problem-solve with your non-ADD child** to reduce or eliminate daily irritations caused by his ADD sib – such as intrusive behavior or taking belongings without permission.

Guideline No. 13

Work together with your partner to tackle the challenges of ADD.

- **Seek ADD parent guidance together.** Working with an experienced ADD family counselor can help both of you to understand what is reasonable to expect of your child with ADD as well as to learn effective ways of dealing with your child's problematic behaviors.

- **Agree upon an approach to parenting.** Working as a team will allow you to be mutually supportive, even when emotions are running high. If you are working together, your child's "divide and conquer" strategy will not be as effective.

- **Help your partner understand how your parenting may be affected by ADD.** For example, you may not always be consistent in your parenting. Work together to create an ADD-friendly atmosphere of support and understanding instead of blame, anger and frustration.

- **Keep the lines of communication open.** This way you'll be better able to support each other and be less reactive in the heat of a difficult situation with your child.

- **Know when to offer and when to ask for help from your partner.** When one parent is under extreme stress, the other parent may need to take over to avert a potentially explosive situation.

Guideline No. 14

Children of divorce with ADD have a "double whammy" to deal with, making it doubly important to try to cooperate and communicate with your former spouse.

It's not always possible to create goodwill and cooperation after a divorce, but it's important to focus on the needs of your kids and try to move past the hurt and anger that so often accompany divorce.

- **Consider working with a family therapist that understands ADD** if attempts to communicate with your ex-spouse are unsuccessful.

- **If your ex-spouse refuses to see a counselor with you,** suggest finding a counselor who can meet with each of you separately for a while.

- **Try to establish the same patterns and expectations in both homes** – predictability and structure will help your child with ADD to function better.

- **Involve your child's father in important child-related meetings** – at school, at the physician's office, and with any counselors or therapists who may be working with your child.

Guideline No. 15

Single moms with ADD need an extra-strong support system.

If you're a single mom with ADD raising a child with ADD, you face a bigger challenge and need more support. Unfortunately, many women in your situation have less support. Here are some strategies other single moms with ADD have used to build a stronger support system:

- **Think about moving closer to people who are sources of emotional support.** For example, one single mom with ADD decided to move back to the town where her parents lived in order to have their support. With two grandparents nearby, she had a backup system if she became sick, if she needed a babysitter, or if she simply needed some precious "down time" from parenting.

- **Find or form a women's ADD support group.** A group of women who understand your feelings and who know the challenges you face can provide moral support and practical advice.

- **Rent a room in your home to a college or graduate student** who can provide specified amounts of child care and can be a welcome second pair of adult hands.

- **Barter child-care with another mom with ADD.**

- **Hire a babysitter for regular time periods once, or better yet, twice a week.** It's important, of course, to hire someone who knows your child and can handle the challenges that your child might pose at times. It's much easier for you to function with established regular times instead of having to make arrangements each time you need or want to go out without your child.

- **Establish regular times to get together with friends.** It's easy to feel so overwhelmed by daily demands that friendships are neglected. Try to set up regular contact – a walk around the neighborhood, a phone call several times a week, an occasional restaurant meal – so that your own emotional needs aren't neglected.

Guideline No. 16

Hold regular family meetings for creative problem-solving.

When everyone participates in finding solutions, each person is more likely to be motivated to change. Regular family meetings can create and reinforce feelings of acceptance and belonging.

Family meetings are a time to discuss issues, plan activities and practice problem-solving. Whether meetings are held on a week-night or weekend, be sure everyone can attend. **"No blaming or complaining"** is the rule. Instead, use this time to come together to focus on solutions, not problems; on progress, not imperfections.

Our Family Meeting Book by Elaine Hightower and Betsy Riley is a great resource to help you structure family meetings. This practical guide offers 52 simple agendas for weekly meetings that are fun and easy for everyone. (see resources)

Guideline No. 17

Focus on the solution, not the problem.

Older children and teens would rather reach their own plan of action instead of being told what to do. Learning how to problem-solve is one of the most important tools you can give your child. It may also be something that you need to practice as well. Family meetings may provide a time to engage in problem-solving together with your children and partner.

Problem-solving is something you can practice together. Challenge your children to not just bring you problems, but to also bring you solutions. This teaches your child to take responsibility for finding answers instead of making excuses for ADD problems.

Guideline No. 18

Teach your children problem-solving techniques

Poor decision making and problem-solving skills are common in people with ADD. In order to improve these skills, it's necessary to practice them often. The following is a plan to work with your child on improving his or her problem-solving skills.

1. **Define the problem.** For example, "My brother keeps taking my things."

2. **Discuss the problem to better understand why it occurs.** It might be productive to invite her brother to join the discussion at this point.

3. **Discuss who is involved in the problem** – and, therefore, in the solution. For example, your daughter might say, "He does it because you never punish him for taking my stuff."

4. **Brainstorm possible solutions to the problem.** At this point, any solutions, no matter how "silly" or ridiculous can be listed:

   a. Put a lock on the door to my room so that I can lock it when I leave.

   b. Tell him he has to stay in his room for a month if he does it again.

   c. Tell him he has to pay me a fine whenever he takes something without permission.

   d. You might suggest an alternate solution, such as "Agree to share your things with him if he stops taking them without permission."

e. You might also suggest, "Your brother feels ignored by you and your friends. Try spending a little time with him every day. He might be more respectful of your private property if he felt you liked him and wanted to spend a little time with him."

5. **Pick a solution to try.** Your daughter might want to try her door-lock solution.

6. **Evaluate the solution after a trial period.** Wait a couple of weeks, then talk to your daughter about the problem. Has it been solved? Partially? Completely? Not at all? Has the problem become worse?

7. **If the solution isn't entirely successful, try to analyze why.** For example, your son may feel angry or resentful that his older sister wants nothing to do with him and locks him out of her room, so he may begin to find other ways to hurt or upset his sister in retaliation.

8. **Modify the solution to fit your analysis.** Your daughter may respond angrily, "He's just a brat. You've got to punish him more, Mom." You might respond, saying, "I know you think that locking him out and punishing him is the right approach, but why don't we try something different. Instead of fighting with your brother and having little to do with him, why not invite him to do something with you sometimes?"

9. **Agree upon the new "solution."** "OK, Mom," your daughter might reluctantly concede. "I'll try to be friendly. But I really think you're just making excuses for him. If this solution

Guideline No. 18

doesn't work, then I think you should punish him when he does stuff like this."

10. **Evaluate the new solution after a trial period.** "You're right, Mom. He hasn't been taking my stuff as much and we seem to be getting along better lately."

11. **Fine tune the solution,** if it's creating positive results. For example, your daughter could talk to her brother and suggest a barter system. "If you want to borrow some of my CDs, then you could do something for me – like wash the dishes this week when it's my turn."

An ADD-friendly Family is a family that finds solutions!

Teach this to your kids, practice it in your family, and your kids will develop a very important skill that will help them throughout their lives.

Guideline No. 19

Reduce family arguments to make room for positive changes.

Many families with ADD fall into a cycle of frustration, fighting and failure. When you can reduce conflicts at home, there's more time for problem-solving and enjoyable family activities. If you feel that you and your child are caught up in frequent arguments over rules and punishments, here are some family-friendly tips:

Draw up a set of household rules. Make sure that the rules are clear and spell out specific behaviors such as:

- No hitting or name-calling.
- No taking other people's property without permission.
- After using something, put it back where it belongs.
- No TV until homework is finished.
- No allowance until all weekly chores are done.

Establish clear consequences for breaking these rules.

- Discuss the consequences for breaking each rule. Everyone should have a say in this discussion. You may be surprised at how fair and insightful your children can be.
- Write down all rules and the consequences for breaking them.
- Display this list prominently in a common area.

This system helps both the parent and child with ADD. The parent is less likely to react impulsively if a clear consequence has been

Guideline No. 19

spelled out beforehand; the child with ADD will be better able to learn desired behaviors when rules and consequences are clear.

Be consistent in applying consequences.

Don't establish consequences you will be reluctant to enforce. A consequence shouldn't be something you threaten when you're in a bad mood and forget when you're in a better mood. A "good" consequence is a reasonable response to an undesired behavior – a teaching tool that will motivate family members to change.

Useful tools for developing programs to manage behaviors through reasonable consequences are provided in:
- *1-2-3: Magic* by Tom Phelan
- *Surviving Your Adolescents* by Tom Phelan

(see resources)

Guideline No. 20

Minimize mother-child conflicts.

When the day is long, frustrations build and conflicts develop. Arguments between parent and child with ADD can rapidly escalate from irritation to out of control yelling. Each reacts to the other, pouring fuel on the fire. Research suggests that mothers and daughters with ADD are particularly prone to arguments and mutual resentment. Here are some ways to minimize conflict and its aftermath.

- **Be sure to find time to be with your child in a loving way each day.**

  - No matter how many conflicts you've had during the day, work hard to find a way to end the day on a better note with your child.

  - Bedtime can be a special bonding time rather than another occasion for argument. Spending a few minutes together, reading or talking, after your child is in bed can calm the turbulent waters of a frustrating day.

Guideline No. 20

- **Try to analyze the patterns of your conflicts so that they can be avoided.**

  - Do each of you try to have the "last word"?

  - When your child yells, is your reaction to yell even louder?

  - Do you and your child seem to take out the day's frustrations on each other?

  - Are your battles centered around homework? Perhaps it would work better if someone else became your child's homework partner – this could be the other parent, a tutor, or even an older teenager.

- **Make conflict avoidance a mutual project.** Talk to your child about arguments and yelling. Tackle it as a team rather than blaming your child. Try to pinpoint the times when arguments are most likely to happen. In many families, angry explosions are more likely around dinner time when everyone feels tired and hungry. Problem-solve together.

  - Would a healthy pre-dinner snack help your child feel calmer?

  - Would you feel more rested and less prone to irritation if you took 15 minutes of "quiet time" before trying to prepare the evening meal?

  - Could you and your child agree to separate and calm down before continuing a discussion that has turned into a fight?

Guideline No. 21

Develop daily routines.

When you are a mother with ADD, it's next to impossible to help your kids develop good daily habits until you learn to develop those habits yourself. Make it a family project, and work with your kids to create better daily family patterns.

Daily life in many families with ADD members can be chaotic. Developing daily routines, particularly a "morning routine" and an "evening routine" can help your family be more orderly. Work on developing these routines as a family and problem-solve as a family when a routine isn't working.

Morning routine

A morning routine begins with getting out of bed and ends with departing for the day's activities. Different family members may have different routines, but they need to be coordinated.

Decide:

- what time each family member should get up in the morning;

- what should be done if that family member oversleeps;

- who needs help getting ready for school and who will help them;

- what time breakfast is served and who prepares it; and

- when each family member should depart.

Guideline No. 21

Problem-solve when the morning routine isn't working smoothly:

- Maybe the "late-sleeper" needs an earlier bedtime.

- Maybe the "can't-find-my-shoes" kid needs to lay out clothes the night before.

- Maybe it would help to have healthy grab-and-go breakfasts available for mornings when someone is running late.

Evening routine

A successful morning routine depends upon a good evening routine. When you make preparations in the evening and get to sleep on time, your morning routine will go more smoothly. An evening routine should specify such things as:

- "Homework time" for each child;

- "Bath time" for each child;

- Preparations to be made for the next day – preparing lunches, setting clothes out, collecting items needed for school;

- "Get in bed time" for each child;

- "Lights out time" for each child;

> More information on developing good habits and routines can be found in: *ADD-friendly Ways to Organize Your Life* by Judith Kolberg and Kathleen Nadeau (see resources)

- And, just as important, "go to sleep" time for Mom.

Many women with ADD sabotage their own morning routines by staying up too late reading or watching TV, then not getting up in time to supervise an organized morning routine for the children.

Guideline No. 22

Don't let your ADD kids become hooked on "electronic reality."

Do your kids complain, "I'm bored," whenever a TV, electronic game, or computer is not available? This is probably because they've had little opportunity to develop other healthier, more desirable activities such as fantasy play, drawing, cooking, building things, reading and making conversation. These activities help your child develop the kinds of neural circuits that will serve her in good stead as she grows up.

Guideline No. 22

"Entertaining yourself" is a skill that a child learns only when the world stops supplying him with non-stop stimulation. Today, many kids, especially those with ADD, have never developed this skill because their time is filled with TV, video games, and the internet. For kids with ADD, electronic stimulation can become addictive. Observe a child with ADD who is suddenly deprived of their Game Boy or TV – the obsession and craving they experience looks a lot like a smoker who is quitting cigarettes "cold turkey."

- **Make sure your child has time to become bored!** When your child feels bored he will have the opportunity and motivation to engage in creative, imaginative, or interactive activities.

- **Supply your children with materials that encourage creativity and problem-solving.** Children have different interests. It's important to have items around that will encourage those interests – such as simple tools and building materials; colored paper, paste, scissors, and felt-tipped markers; items needed to cook a favorite recipe; and games that require concentration and strategy. An older child might enjoy learning to use a camera – make sure that it's an older camera that will be a small loss if your ADD child accidentally damages it.

Activities involving tools, scissors, painting or cooking should also always be performed under the supervision of an adult.

- **Look for clubs, teams and organizations that will encourage your child to be more active and develop social skills and coordination skills.** Scouting, athletics and church groups are often good settings for a child who needs structure to develop people skills and coordination skills.

- **Don't pull the plug on your child's electronic world all at once.** If your kids are plugged into "electronic reality" nearly full time, it's not realistic to stop everything at once. For example, if your child is used to watching TV after school, as well as in the evening, let that pattern continue, but begin to whittle down TV time. You might begin to wean your child from TV watching by setting a one-hour limit in the afternoon and a second one-hour limit in the evening.

- **Help your child be selective in TV watching.** Instead of flopping down on the couch to watch whatever happens to be playing, help your child to become more selective. Just as few people would select a book at random, it's important for your child to actively choose a TV program rather than passively "zone out" in front of the TV.

- **Make TV and video games a time-limited, earned activity.** In many families, kids are given unlimited access to TV or electronic games, which are sometimes taken away as a punishment for misbehavior. Instead, turn this pattern on its head. Make TV and electronic games a special, time-limited activity that is earned after completing more desirable activities – homework, reading, chores, outdoor exercise.

Guideline No. 23

Teach your older kids how to deal with internet distractions.

For older kids, the internet and access to "instant messages" from friends can become a powerful distraction. Many middle and high school teens work on computers to do homework. Too often the result is spending most of their time "IM-ing" friends and little time on homework. Here are some tips for managing appropriate internet use:

- **Keep the computer connected to the internet in a "public" space within your house** – the kitchen, breakfast room, or family room might be good choices depending upon the layout of your home. That way, when your teen needs to go on the internet to do research for homework, they'll be less prone to wander from homework to off-task behaviors.

- **Have your child do homework on a computer that is not connected to the internet.** Instant-messaging friends online is a very strong temptation for most teenagers. It's the 21st century version of "talking on the phone all night" that tempted earlier generations of teens. It may not be realistic to expect your teen to resist this temptation while working on a computer that is online. Instead of setting up a situation that will create temptation and conflict, have your teen work offline and then use a period of online communication with friends as a treat at the end of the evening after homework is completed.

Guideline No. 24

For ADD strategies to succeed you need support and structure.

Support –

- Look for support from family members, friends, ADD support groups, ADD coaches and professional organizers.

- Seek understanding, encouragement and camaraderie as you tackle the hard work of learning to manage the ADD challenges of daily life.

- You may need more support as you begin to make changes; later, you may be able to operate more independently.

- Remember: a housekeeper is cheaper than a divorce.

Structure –

It comes in many forms: creating realistic to-do lists; setting do-able goals; learning to select smaller tasks and then staying with them to completion; and developing reminder systems that will work for you.

Guideline No. 25

To get things done, create a "Must List" and a "Master List."

If you're like many other women with ADD, you've got lists scribbled everywhere, but no system for getting your "to-do's" done. Instead of scribbles and scraps, try using a two-list system: a "Must List" and a "Master List."

- **Make a short daily "Must List" – then get it done.** Only write on today's list what *must* be done today. These things take priority over everything else, unless there's an emergency.

- **Set a daily goal to complete your "Must List."** Keep shortening your "Must List" until you reach your daily goal. If you rarely complete your "Must List" you are either over-committed or need help to decide what *must* be done. A counselor, ADD coach or professional organizer can help you set priorities and reduce over-commitment.

- **Keep a "Master List" where you write all things that need to be done, now and in the future.** Review your master list each day and decide which items should be transferred to today's "Must List."

- **Keep both lists together and with you at all times.**

- **Help your kids learn to keep a to-do list.** Gradually teach them to keep track of their own "to-do's" instead of always relying on you to remind them.

Guideline No. 26

Look for creative solutions to "take care of business" while raising kids with ADD.

When you're a mother with ADD, who struggles with distractibility, and your kids with ADD create non-stop distractions, it can seem impossible to get anything done. Kids with ADD are often impatient and demanding. If they have a question, they want an answer <u>now</u>. Their voices can be loud and hard to ignore. And kids with ADD need more structure and supervision, so it's rare that they can function independently for long. So what can a mother with ADD do when she needs to concentrate? It's never easy, but here are some tips:

- **Early morning "Island of Peace."** One mother became an "early bird," getting up at least an hour before the rest of the family. She described her morning time as her "island of peace" before the storm of the day. This hour was her time to plan, prioritize, and take care of any paperwork that needed to be mailed or sent to school that day.

- **Go be a kid!** Another mother used the phrase, "Go be a kid!" to let her children know it was time to go outside or into the family room and give her some uninterrupted peace. It's important to have a safe place (a fenced yard area if your children are younger and want to play outside), where you can keep an eye on them without having them underfoot. While your children are busy "being kids" you'll have time to make a

few uninterrupted phone calls, jot down a grocery list, sort through the mail, or relax for a few precious minutes.

- **Mom's Quiet time.** Teach your kids that "Mom needs 'quiet time'." Even young children can learn to give you a few quiet, uninterrupted moments if you train them on a daily basis, rewarding each child who has not interrupted you during "quiet time."

- **Kids' Quiet Time.** And teach them that kids need quiet time too. Quiet time in their room engaging in a low-key, enjoyable activity is good for kids with ADD and helps them "decompress" when they're over-stimulated. Teaching kids about 'quiet time' – both yours and theirs – is an important lesson in learning to live well with ADD.

- **Create a "traveling desk".** Use a zippered, fabric shoulder bag to neatly store your checkbook, stamps, pen, address book, paperclips, felt-tip marker, etc. Within your "traveling desk" keep one zip-closured see-through plastic folder to store bills to be paid. (Zip-closure is important so that nothing can fall out.) Keep another zip-closured folder for other paperwork. Then, when bills or other paperwork arrive in the mail, or when kids bring forms from school that need to be completed, store them in your "traveling desk."

- **Use your lunch hour at work for home management.** Try doing personal paperwork at work during your lunch hour. Bring your traveling desk to work each day. Many women find that they have more energy in the middle of the day to pay bills, balance the checkbook, or write a letter than they have late in the evening.

- **Use 'waiting time' to do paperwork.** If you're like many moms, you spend a big chunk of your week taking kids to lessons and sports practices. If you have your "traveling desk," waiting time in doctor's or dentist's offices are also a great time to get paperwork done.

- **Tag team with your partner.** If you have a spouse or significant other, who is a parent figure in your family, coordinate with your partner so that you each have uninterrupted time to take care of tasks that require concentration.

Guideline No. 27

Learn ADD-friendly organizing strategies, and teach them to your kids.

An ADD-friendly strategy is one that works <u>with</u> your ADD, not against it. Here are a few ADD-friendly tips:

- Do it as soon as you think of it.

- A short list is better than a long memory.

- Don't just tell me, write it down.

- Put it where you can't forget it.

- Think like a restaurant server – pick up and put away as you move from room to room.

For more information on getting better organized see:
- *ADD-friendly Ways to Organize Your Life* by Judith Kolberg and Kathleen Nadeau
- *Making Peace with the Things in Your Life* by Cindy Glovinsky

(see resources)

Guideline No. 28

ADD-friendly ways to organize family activities and schedules.

Keeping track of everyone's schedule in today's busy family often feels impossible. But don't give up! Families need an organizer, too! Whether it's a family calendar, or a household or family notebook, these simple ideas can save time, cut stress, and enhance communication in any family or household.

- **Set up a single large monthly calendar on which each member of the family logs in his or her schedule.** Each person is responsible to enter or check that all activities and appointments are listed. By completing the calendar at the beginning of each month, conflicts will become apparent and changes can be made early on, instead of at the last minute. (Kids will need a reminder and guidance to do this.)

- **Post the calendar in a common location such as the kitchen or family room.** Make it a habit to have family members check the calendar each morning as they come into the kitchen to plan for the day ahead and again in the evening to plan for tomorrow.

Guideline No. 28

- **Use a wipe-off message board** for last minute changes in the schedule and to let others in the family know where you have gone. You can also use it to post phone messages.

- **Create a three-ringed family or household notebook to contain all pertinent family information:** pizza menus and business cards, school hand-outs and church bulletins, class, carpool and soccer schedules and scout camp brochures. Each member of the family should be familiar with all information contained in the notebook and refer to it when necessary. Basic organizer forms for creating your Household Notebook can be downloaded free at *www.organizedhome.com*

Websites to find help to organize and schedule your whole family:
www. organizedhome.com
www. thefamilyplanner.com

More information on how structure and support can help you take charge of ADD for yourself and your family can be found in:
ADD-friendly Ways to Organize Your Life by Judith Kolberg and Kathleen Nadeau
(see resources)

- **Keep your Household Notebook near the family's main telephone and family calendar** to help organize family activities and guide scheduling decisions.

Guideline No. 29

ADD-friendly room clean-up routines for kids.

Getting your kids to clean up their rooms is a tough and often losing battle. If you're a mom with ADD yourself, you probably feel overwhelmed by trying to keep the rest of the house in some semblance of order. Arguing with your kids about cleaning up their rooms may feel like more trouble than it's worth. And it's hard to point a finger at your kids if your own bedroom is piled high with clothes you haven't hung up and other clutter. So what can make things better, for you and your kids? Here are some ADD-friendly tips:

Guideline No. 29

- **Keep each other company during cleanup** – Often all that your child needs is a little company (having someone there provides built-in structure) and a little support. Don't do the work for your child, but give your child suggestions such as: "Remember, the socks  go in the top drawer." or "All the balls go in the red box and the hats go on the top shelf."

- **Make it a family affair** – talk to your kids about "clean up time" – let them know that it's hard for you too and work on it together.

  - Set a time for room clean-up

  - Then set a timer for thirty minutes (one half-hour is easy to survive!)

  - Make a game of it – have a clean-up challenge – see who can make the most progress in room clean up in 30 minutes.

  - Award an immediate prize – a favorite activity, favorite dessert, etc.
    (Make sure that everyone gets an award for working on room clean-up, but give the "winner" a bigger award.)

Guideline No. 30

Conquering chaos the ADD-friendly way.

- **Don't bite off more than you can chew!** Break organizing efforts into "chewable" bites that you can do from start to finish without stopping.

  - One shelf at a time

  - One drawer at a time

- **To get it done, make it fun!**

  - Energize yourself and your child with upbeat music.

  - Make a game of it – make "bets" on how much each of you can accomplish in 15 minutes – see which one of you was more accurate, which one accomplished more.

- **Get your child to help YOU de-clutter** – don't just focus on THEIR mess.

- **Help your child de-clutter in return** – it's more fun doing it together!

- **Reward yourself and your child IMMEDIATELY** – this will link organizing activities with a positive experience – create a "special time" with your child as a reward for "digging out" activities.

Guideline No. 31

Help your child downsize the ADD-friendly way.

Whether child or adult, people with ADD tend to hang onto "too much stuff." This happens for several reasons:

1. People with ADD often have many interests that they impulsively pursue for short periods of time and then drop when a new interest comes along.

2. There's no established "time" to downsize. Things just accumulate, pile up, and then become overwhelming to deal with.

3. Because decision-making can be difficult, it's hard to decide what to keep and how much to keep.

What can help your child to downsize?

1. **Clutter Bags** – Give your child a "clutter bag" that "lives" in her closet. Leave the bag there until it fills up.

2. **Downsizing Depot** – Then take it to the family "downsizing depot" – a designated area in the basement, storage room, or garage where de-cluttering items are kept before giving away.

3. **De-clutter as you clean.** Make de-cluttering a routine part of cleaning up – teach your child to ask herself how much she really uses each item that she picks up to put away. If the answer is "hardly ever," that's an obvious item to put in her "clutter bag."

4. **"Age" your child's clutter.** It's very hard, even for many adults, to give something away "forever" because so many dreams and memories are often attached to each item that we own. So, instead of throwing things away immediately, "age" your child's clutter. Have your child put rarely used items in her "clutter bag" and promise her that the items will be saved, not thrown away. Six months or a year later your child will feel much less attached to these items and will more easily part from them.

5. **Develop a "Me Museum" with Your Child** – Museum's don't keep and display everything. They carefully examine items and then save only the best for exhibits. Play a museum game with your child. Your child can be the museum curator of the "Me Museum". At the end of each school year, make a fun project out of saving the "best" of that year for the "Me Museum" – this might involve a favorite outfit that your child has outgrown, favorite art work, special school projects, and photographs. Items for the "Me Museum" should be carefully boxed and labeled – for example, "Annie's Fourth Grade Year." Then other items that aren't the "best" can go in the "Clutter Bag" and age for a while.

Guideline No. 32

Create an ADD-friendly bedroom with your child.

To take charge of ADD, you'll need to develop new habits. New habits are never easy, but here are some tips to help you and your child. Make sure your child's bedroom is:

- NOT filled with "too much stuff"

- Has a bed that is "easy to make"

- Is cheerful and colorful

- Has storage units that are clearly labeled and easy to use.

Here are some tips for making your child's bedroom more ADD-friendly:

- **Creative crates** – Try using clearly labeled, colorful, open storage boxes instead of dresser drawers. For example, purchase colorful plastic milk crates and label each one:

    Socks,
    Underwear,
    Tops,
    Bottoms,
    Jackets,
    Sweatshirts,
    Shoes

    For younger children, use pictures instead of labels.

    Line up the milk cartons on open shelves that are far enough apart to allow your child to toss items into the appropriate milk crate.

- **Easily made beds** – Want your child to make her bed each morning? Get your child fitted sheets, pillow cases, and a comforter that match. Don't bother with a top sheet. Then all your child needs to do is pull up the comforter in one fell swoop – no matter if the pillow is under or on top of the comforter – the bed will look neat and can be made quickly no matter how rushed your child's morning routine.

- **User-friendly closets.** Place laundry basket (for dirty clothes), milk crate for pajamas, and milk crate for shoes in close proximity to one another. For example, you could build a waist-high closet shelf with room for the laundry basket below, and a milk crate for pajamas above. Help your child develop the habit of undressing in front of the open closet. All your child needs to do is – take off clothes, toss them in the laundry basket, and grab the pajamas that "live" on the shelf above … position a "shoe crate" just outside for sneakers … after socks are tossed in the laundry basket.

Guideline No. 33

Develop new habits the ADD-friendly way.

New habits take time to develop. Here are some tips to help you and your child get started.

- **Tie a new habit to an old one.** For example, if your habit is to enter your house by the kitchen door and you want to develop a new habit of always putting your keys in the same place, choose a convenient spot near the kitchen door to place a key hook; then tie the two habits together – "open the door, hang up the keys."

- **Make the new habit as easy as possible.** Don't place the key hook far from the kitchen door.

- **Make the new habit hard to ignore.** Create a large, impossible-to-miss sign that asks, "Did you hang up your keys?"

- **Put reminders everywhere.** Put another reminder in the hallway, another upstairs. Post as many as you need until you've developed the new habit.

- **Visualize yourself doing the new habit.** "Practice" in your mind walking in the door and hanging your keys on the hook.

- **Make "instant corrections."** Go back and hang your keys on the hook the instant you realize you've forgotten, even if it's inconvenient.

- **Problem–solve if it's not working.** If you still forget to hang up your keys, problem-solve. Maybe you'll be more successful if your key hook is near the place where you put your purse or your briefcase.

- **Problem-solve with your family.** Other family members may have useful ideas. Asking for suggestions to help with ADD struggles is good role-modeling for your kids.

For more information on ADD-friendly habit development, see:
ADD-friendly Ways to Organize Your Life
by Judith Kolberg and Kathleen Nadeau
(see resources)

Guideline No. 34

Combat clutter to create calm.

Many women with ADD live with a constantly cluttered environment, and ADD clutter tends to multiply. If you haven't sorted through yesterday's mail, you're more likely to just toss today's mail on top of the pile and let the clutter grow. Here are a few ADD-friendly rules to combat clutter:

- **First, clutter no more.** Before you tackle existing clutter, start by creating no "new" clutter. Hang up your clothes, sort and process your mail, put things back after using them, put groceries in the pantry, fold the laundry and put it away, wash the dishes and put them away.

- **Think small.** Don't take on too much at once – take on "one drawer per day," or "one shelf per day."

- **Finish what you start.** Take on one small organizing project at a time and then stick with it to completion.

- **Don't try to do it alone.** You and your kids can work on this together. Ask your kids for ideas and help with your clutter; offer them support in digging out their rooms. Give your children the message that, with ADD, being organized doesn't come naturally, but together we can do it.

Guideline No. 35

Collaborate and communicate with your child's school.

Teamwork between home and school is critical. It is important that the school faculty be aware of all that you are doing for your child with ADD. That way, everyone is working toward the common goal of helping your child achieve independence and academic success. The school will need information about your child's diagnosis, treatment and academic recommendations so that a plan of action can be set in place.

It is critical to establish consistent and open communication with your child's teacher. Collaborate with your child's teacher to find solutions for your child's ADD challenges.

With your busy schedule, it's not always easy to meet with your child's teacher in person. Here are some ways to keep in touch:

- **Communicate by phone or email on a regular basis.**

- **Create a notebook that travels back and forth with your child.** This allows the teacher to write down any notes about your child. You can also add any important information that you think the teacher should be aware of as it arises.

- **Provide the teacher with a set of stamped, self-addressed envelopes.** The teacher may use them to mail important information home rather than sending it with your child, who may lose it or forget it.

Guideline No. 36

Learn strategies to reduce homework hassles.

Let your child take an active role in making homework decisions. Homework isn't optional, but there are many options about when and how to do homework.

- **Help your child observe himself or herself so that the child learns when and how he or she works best.** Some kids need vigorous exercise after school, while others need to "veg-out" before tackling homework. Still others do better if they complete homework before dinner. Some need to work in the same room with a parent to stay on track. There are kids who concentrate best while listening to music; others need total silence.

- **Encourage your child to try different approaches to homework.** Together with your child, develop a daily homework plan that best suits his or her individual needs. Then encourage your child to stick to the plan until it becomes a habit.

> For more information on ways to make the daily homework battle go more smoothly see: *How to do Homework without Throwing Up* by Trevor Romain (see resources)

- **Remove distractions that interfere with homework completion.** Whether it's television, the phone or instant email messages, anything that repeatedly interferes with homework should be removed until homework is finished.

- **If your child takes medication, it's important that he or she be on the medication during homework and after-school activities.** Be sure that he or she schedules difficult reading assignments and written work for times when the medication is most effective.

- **Don't try to "tutor" your child.** That doesn't mean that you can't help your child once in a while. But if your child needs a lot of help, has a specific learning disability or has major problems with planning, time management and completion of long-term assignments, he or she needs professional help.

- **Don't do the work *for* your child.** By spending many hours helping your child, and/or doing much of the work for him or her, you are not allowing the child to learn to deal with her ADD. Give your child support and encouragement, along with the message that he or she is strong enough to carry the load.

Guideline No. 37

Make ADD treatment a family affair.

When family members have ADD, everyone in the family is affected. Taking charge of ADD works best when the whole family is learning together.

Spouses and siblings who don't have ADD need a chance to learn about ADD and to play a role in finding family solutions to ADD problems. Not every family member will be involved in each step of treatment, but no one should be left out of the process.

Medication – Adults and children respond to the same types of medications for the treatment of ADD. Stimulants and newer non-stimulant medications such as atomoxetine have proven to be safe and effective. Keep in mind that ADD is a quality of life disorder that affects you 24 hours a day in your daily activities as well as your sleep patterns.

Because many women have long days, new long-acting medications are often best, helping you to be more efficient and productive throughout the day and evening. Many women with ADD also need medication to treat a co-existing condition such as anxiety or depression.

When a mother takes medication for ADD, her child will tend to be more receptive to taking medication as well. When both mother and child are taking effective doses of appropriate medication, family life will run more smoothly.

ADD-focused psychotherapy – Look for a therapist who works with adults on individual concerns as well as on parenting and family issues related to ADD. To be effective, psychotherapy for ADD should focus on helping you to find solutions to daily life management problems, to understand and accept yourself and to improve the quality of your relationships with friends and family.

Parent/family counseling – Make sure that your family counselor understands how you are impacted by ADD and teaches ADD-friendly parenting techniques. Both parents should participate in parent counseling. At times, it's important to include the whole family. Being the partner, child or sibling of someone with ADD is challenging too. Everyone in the family should take part in finding ADD family-friendly solutions.

ADD-coaching – A skilled ADD coach can help you set realistic goals, problem-solve and stay on track as your work to make changes. A coach can also work with your children – helping them identify problems, brain-storm solutions and put those solutions into action.

Professional organizing – When you're trying to get from overwhelmed to organized, a professional organizer can work wonders, working with you in a hands-on fashion to sort and organize your household. Some professional organizers work with parents and children together, making it a family project.

Guideline No. 38

To put it all together, take it one step at a time.

If you're like most ADD families, there are lots of areas that need to be organized or changed. Be careful not to take on too many projects at once. Build on your successes, one step at a time.

Spouses, teachers, siblings, grandparents . . . coaches, organizers, therapists and physicians . . . they are all part of the ADD-friendly environment necessary to ensure success for you and your child with ADD. Together you can learn to love your life and achieve great things.

Resources

Resources to help you understand and cope with your ADD

A Housekeeper is Cheaper Than a Divorce by Kathy Fitzgerald Sherman. Available from Advantage Books for $19.95.

View from the Cliff by Lynn Weiss, Ph.D. Available from Taylor Trade Publishing for $15.95.

Attention Deficit Disorder in Adults by Dr. Lynn Weiss. Available from Taylor Publishing Company for $12.95.

ADD-Friendly Ways to Organize Your Life by Judith Kolberg and Kathleen Nadeau, Ph.D. Available from Advantage Books for $21.95.

Understanding Women with ADD, edited by Kathleen G. Nadeau, Ph.D. and Patricia O. Quinn, M.D. Available from Advantage Books for $19.95.

Moms with ADD by Christine Adamec. Available from Advantage Books for $14.95.

ADD in the Workplace by Kathleen G. Nadeau, Ph.D. Available from Advantage Books for $29.95.

What Does Everybody Else Know That I Don't? by Michelle Novonti, Ph.D. Available from Advantage Books for $14.95.

ADD and Romance by Jonathan Scott Halverstadt, M.S. Available from Advantage Books for $13.95.

Finding a Career That Works for You by Wilma R. Fellman, M.Ed., LPC. Available from Independent Publishers Group for $16.95.

Adventures in Fast Forward by Kathleen G. Nadeau, Ph.D. Available from Advantage Books for $23.95.

ADD on the Job by Dr. Lynn Weiss. Available from Cooper Square Publishing for $13.95.

Making Peace with the Things in Your Life by Cindy Glovinsky, ACSW. Available from St. Martin's Press for $14.95.

Gender Issues and ADHD edited by Patricia Quinn, M.D. and Kathleen Nadeau, Ph.D. Available from Advantage Books for $39.00.

Women with ADD by Sari Solden. Available from Advantage Books for $11.95.

Resources to help you parent your ADD child

Raise Your Child's Social IQ by Cathi Cohen, L.C.S.W. Available from Advantage Books for $14.95.

Understanding Girls with ADD by Kathleen G. Nadeau, Ph.D., Ellen B. Littman, Ph.D., and Patricia O. Quinn, M.D. Available from Advantage Books for $19.95.

1-2-3 Magic by Thomas W. Phelan, Ph. D. Available from Child Management, Inc, for $12.95.

ADD & Driving by J. Marlene Snyder, Ph.D. Available from Whitefish Consulting for $17.00.

Dr. Larry Silver's Advice to Parents on ADD by Larry B. Silver, M.D. Available from Three Rivers Press for $19.00.

Surviving Your Adolescents by Thomas W. Phelan, Ph.D. Available from Parent Magic for $13.00.

From Chaos to Calm by Janet E. Heininger, Ph.D. and Sharon K. Weiss, M.Ed. Available from Advantage Books for $14.95.

Our Family Meeting Book by Elaine Hightower and Betsy Riley. Available from Free Spirit Publishing for $16.95.

Resources to help your child understand and live with his or her ADD

How To Do Homework Without Throwing Up by Trevor Romain. Available from Free Spirit Publishing for $8.95.

Learning to Slow Down and Pay Attention by Kathleen G. Nadeau, Ph.D. and Ellen B. Dixon, Ph.D. Illustrated by John R. Rose. Available from Advantage Books for $10.95.

"Putting on the Brakes" by Patricia O. Quinn, M.D. and Judith M. Stern, M.A. (Also available in Spanish.) Both are available from Advantage Books for $9.95.

The "Putting on the Brakes" Activity Book by Patricia O. Quinn, M.D. and Judith M. Stern, M.A. Illustrated by Neil Russell. Available from Advantage Books for $14.95.

The Best of "Brakes" Activity Book by Patricia O. Quinn and Judith M. Stern, M.A. Illustrated by Kate Sternberg. Available from Advantage Books for $14.95.

Resources to help your older child cope with his or her ADD

Adolescents and ADD by Patricia O. Quinn, M.D. Available from Advantage Books for $12.95.

Help4ADD@High School by Kathleen G. Nadeau, Ph.D. Available from Advantage Books for $15.95.

ADD and the College Student by Patricia O. Quinn, M.D. Available from Advantage Books for $14.95.

Survival Guide for College Students with ADD or LD by Kathleen G. Nadeau, Ph.D. Available from Advantage Books for $9.95.

Learning Outside the Lines by Jonathan Mooney and David Cole. Available from Fireside Books for $13.00.

Organizations that provide help to families with ADD

National Center for Gender Issues and AD/HD
3268 Arcadia Pl NW
Washington, DC 20015
Telephone: (888) 238-8588
Fax: (202) 966-1561
www.ncgiadd.org

A nonprofit organization that advocates for women and girls with AD/HD. Site includes articles specifically focused on the unique issues faced by women and girls. Membership includes ADDvance News Online, a monthly electronic newsletter, a discount on books sold on its website and discounts to events and conferences sponsored by the National Center.

National Attention Deficit Disorder Association (ADDA)
P.O. Box 543
Pottstown, PA 19464
Telephone: (484) 945-2101
Fax: (610) 970-7520
www.add.org

A nonprofit advocacy organization that focuses on issues of teens, adults and families with ADD. Membership includes a bi-monthly newsletter, *Focus*, and discounts at the annual national meeting.

Children and Adults with Attention-Deficit/Hyperactivity Disorder (CHADD)
8181 Professional Place, Suite 201
Landover, MD 20785
Telephone: (800) 233-4050
Fax: (301) 306-7090
www.chadd.org.

A national advocacy organization for children and adults with ADD, CHADD has a highly informative website with scientifically accurate information as well as an online bookstore. CHADD also maintains a federally funded ADD resource center staffed by individuals available to answer your questions and to help you find the resources that you need.

ADD Resources
223 Tacoma Avenue, South #100
Tacoma, WA 98402
www.addresources.org

Website for this rapidly growing national non-profit provides 85 free articles by national ADHD authorities, over 100 links to ADD-related websites, a National ADHD Directory which lists over 715 service providers, and a free monthly eNews as well as ADHD Skills Building Telecourses. Their mission is to help people with ADHD achieve their full potential.

About the Authors

Dr. Patricia Quinn is a developmental pediatrician in the Washington, D.C., area. A graduate of the Georgetown University Medical School, she specializes in child development and psychopharmacology. Dr. Quinn has worked for more than 30 years in the areas of ADD and learning disabilities. She gives workshops nationwide and has appeared on Lifetime TV's New Attitudes, the PBS show, To the Contrary, and on Good Morning America discussing the issue of women with ADHD. Dr. Quinn appeared in the video aired on PBS titled, OUTSIDE IN: A Look at Adults with Attention Deficit Disorder.

For the last decade, Dr. Quinn has devoted her attention professionally to the issues confronting girls and women with ADHD. Her 1999 book, *Understanding Girls with ADHD*, was co-authored with Drs. Nadeau and Littman and is groundbreaking in its presentation of this population. She was also co-editor of *ADDvance: A Magazine for Women with ADD* and is co-founder and currently the director of the non-profit organization, the National Center for Gender Issues and ADHD. In 2002, Dr. Quinn co-edited with her partner, Dr. Nadeau, two volumes on these important topics, *Understanding Women with ADHD* and the only text for clinicians, *Gender Issues and ADHD: Research, Diagnosis, and Treatment.*

Dr. Quinn lives in Washington, D.C., with her husband and four children, three of whom have ADD. She, herself, has ADD and relates that she has enjoyed almost every minute of it. She may be contacted by calling or faxing (202) 966-1561. All of her books may be ordered through Advantage Books by calling (888)-238-8588 or purchased online at www.addvance.com.

Dr. Kathleen Nadeau, a clinical psychologist, earned her doctoral degree at the University of Florida in 1970 and has practiced in the Washington, D.C., area throughout her professional career, specializing in treating children and adults with ADD and related conditions. Dr. Nadeau offers lectures and workshops across the United States, and has also given presentations on ADD in Denmark, Norway, Germany, Puerto Rico and Japan. She has appeared on national television broadcasts both in the U.S. and in Japan and appeared in the video aired on PBS titled, OUTSIDE IN: A Look at Adults with Attention Deficit Disorder.

For the last decade, Dr. Nadeau has focused on the issues confronting girls and women with ADD. She co-authored with Drs. Quinn and Littman the ground-breaking book *Understanding Girls with AD/HD*, and co-edited with Dr. Quinn the books *Understanding Women with AD/HD* and *Gender Issues and AD/HD*. Together, she and

Dr. Quinn co-edited *ADDvance, A Magazine for Women with ADD*, and co-founded the National Center for Gender Issues and ADHD.

Today, Dr. Nadeau continues her collaborative work with Dr. Quinn in lectures and publications.

Dr. Nadeau is the director of the Chesapeake Center for Attention and Learning Disorders, a private clinic that specializes in the diagnosis and treatment of individuals of all ages with ADD and associated disorders. She lives with her husband in suburban Maryland. Dr. Nadeau has ADD and has raised a daughter with the disorder. She is best known for her insightful, practical advice on surviving and thriving with ADD – counsel that has developed out of both her personal and clinical experience. Dr. Nadeau can be contacted at (301) 562-8448. All of her books may be ordered through Advantage Books by calling (888) 238-8588 or online at www.addvance.com.